D0764212

GLACIER
National Park

by Ruth Radlauer

Design and photographs
by Rolf Zillmer

AN ELK GROVE BOOK

 CHILDRENS PRESS, CHICAGO

The author and photographer thank
Glacier National Park personnel
for their help with photography
and manuscript authentication.

Photo credits:
Mountain Goats, page 19 (top) by Doug Chadwick
Ptarmigan, page 27 by Robert Gildart
Grizzly Bear, page 33 by Danny On

Library of Congress Cataloging in Publication Data

Radlauer, Ruth.
    Glacier National Park.

    "An Elk Grove book."
    SUMMARY: Introduces Glacier National Park, which
has nearly fifty small glaciers. Includes discus-
sions of the bighorn sheep and hiking and camping
in the Park.
        1. Glacier National Park—Juvenile literature.
[1. Glacier National Park. 2. National parks and reserves]
I. Zillmer, Rolf. II. Title.
F737.G5R32   917.86'52   76-48993
ISBN 0-516-07491-1

3 4 5 6 7 8 9 10 11 12 13 14 15 R 83 82 81

Contents

What is Glacier National Park?

There are almost 50 small glaciers in Glacier National Park. But the park was not named for them. It was named for the towering peaks and ridges carved by huge glaciers of the ice age. This great scenery was carved during the last three million years.

Glacier National Park is a search for bighorn sheep when you hike the Highline Trail. It's the roar of hundreds of waterfalls made by melting snow. It's the echo of a pebble dropped into a glacial crevasse.

Glacier National Park is the many blues of 200 sparkling lakes. It's the spatter of red, yellow, and pink flowers hiding a ground squirrel in an alpine meadow of Logan Pass.

This park is a horseback ride in the forest, a boat ride on Waterton Lake, a nature walk with a Ranger.

Along with Waterton Lakes National Park of Canada, Glacier is part of the world's first International Peace Park. Straddling the U.S. and Canadian border, the park stands as a symbol of friendship between two countries.

Part of Grinnell Glacier

St. Mary Lake

Bighorn Sheep

Wild Flowers Hide A Ground Squirrel

Waterton Lake From Bear's Hump

Your Trip to Glacier National Park

Waterton-Glacier International Peace Park is in the Rocky Mountains. The park stretches from northwest Montana across the international border into Canada.

By air you fly to Kalispell or Great Falls, Montana, and take a bus or drive a rented car to the park. The train takes you to East Glacier or to Belton near West Glacier. If your family drives, the park is on U.S. Highways 2 and 89, reached from U.S. Highways 91 and 93. Canadian Highways 5 and 6 in Alberta lead to the Waterton entrance.

For your trip you should take good hiking shoes or boots, long pants, sun hat, rain wear, and clothes for cold nights. Later in this book you'll find out why you also need bells to tie on your belt or pack.

Pets must be on leashes at all times, and they're not allowed on trails or in the backcountry. So your pet monkey, dog, or cat may be happier at home.

Write to the Superintendent at West Glacier, Montana, 59936 for maps and information to help you plan your trip.

Hwy. 6

Hwy. 5

◄ WATERTON LAKES NATIONAL PARK

Red Rock Canyon

Bear's Hump Trail

Waterton Lakes
Information Centre

Miles	0		5		10		15
Kilometers	0	6	12	18	24		

BRITISH COLUMBIA   CANADA

MONTANA   UNITED STATES

ALBERTA   CANADA
MONTANA   UNITED STATES

Cameron Lake

Kintla Lake

Continental Divide

Flathead River (Middle Fork)

Bowman Lake

GLACIER NATIONAL PARK

MANY GLACIER

Hwy. 17

Hwy. 89

Babb

Quartz Lake

Iceberg Lake
Swiftcurrent Lake

Sherburne Lake
Josephine Lake

Grinnell Glacier
Highline Trail

Grinnell Lake

Visitor Center
St. Mary

Logging Lake

Mt. Oberlin
Hidden Lake Overlook
Going-to-the-Sun-Road
Trail of Cedars
Moose Country

Garden Wall
Haystack Butte
Logan Pass

Polebridge

Saint Mary Lake

Mt. Reynolds

Sun Point Nature Trail

Camas Creek Entrance

Avalanche Lake

CUT BANK

Huckleberry Mountain
Fire Ecology Trail

Lake McDonald

Sperry Glacier

Hwy. 89

Kiowa
To Great Falls
Hwy. 89

Sperry Chalets

Gunsight Pass Trail

TWO MEDICINE

Flinsch Peak

APGAR

Information Center
Park Headquarters

McDonald Creek

West Glacier

Hwy. 2

Flathead River (North Fork)

Two Medicine Lake
East Glacier Park

Hwy. 49

Hwy. 2

River

N

Flathead

To Flathead Lake

To Kalispell

Hwy. 2

	Campground	⚑
	Railroad	+++++
	Paved Road	——
	Dirt Road	– – –
	Trail	······

⚑ WALTON

Walton Goat Lick

BLACKFEET INDIAN RESERVATION

To Build a Mountain

The peaks and valleys of Glacier National Park are part of the Rocky Mountains that reach from Canada to New Mexico. The rocks in these peaks tell a story that began one billion years ago. This area was a flat place that began to sink slowly, only a few inches a year. As the land sank, water covered it to make a shallow sea.

Into this shallow sea, rivers poured silt, mud, and sand. Layers and layers of mud and sand settled on the bottom of the sea. The land kept sinking and more layers formed. Under great weight, the layers turned to stone.

Volcanoes forced hot, molten rock, or lava, up through the sea bottom. In the water, the lava cooled into blobs now called pillow lava.

Then the land began to rise. Some force made the earth fold the way a rug wrinkles when you push against it with your foot. Pushed from west to east, the layers were uplifted, folded, and broken. During a period of millions of years this great force pushed the layers thousands of feet into the sky to make the Rocky Mountains.

Ripples In Sandstone Formed In Sand At The Bottom Of A Sea

Layers of Sandstone

What Force Lifted These Layers Toward The Sky?

Erosion, the Great Carver

As the rocks were lifted to make mountains, erosion began to wear them down. Tiny plants called lichen grew on the rocks and made weak acids that ate slowly into them. Water in cracks froze and made the cracks wider. Bits of sand and dead plants formed soil in the cracks and made a place for trees and bushes to grow. As the trees grew, their roots broke the rocks apart even more. Little by little, some of the rocks became soil. Over thousands of years, wind carried soil away and rivers cut V-shaped valleys.

Then, three million years ago, the ice age began. During this time, snow filled the valleys and almost hid the mountains. Very little snow melted before new snow fell. It packed into huge hunks of ice four and five thousand feet thick.

The weight of these huge masses of ice caused them to slide slowly down the mountainsides. As they slid, they picked up rocks and boulders that scraped the earth. The moving masses of ice often carved U-shaped valleys like those you see today in Glacier National Park.

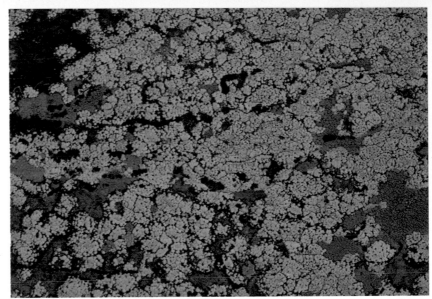

This Lichen Grows On Rock

Trees And Bushes Grow In Cracks

Glaciers Carve Too

A mass of packed snow that doesn't move is a snowfield. But huge masses of ice that move down a slope are called glaciers.

Like a giant bulldozer, a glacier slowly pushes rocks and earth aside as it goes. The piles of rock the glacier pushes aside are called lateral (side) moraines. The pile the glacier pushes ahead is called a terminal (end) moraine. Some lateral moraines become mountain ridges like Snyder and Howe Ridges near Lake McDonald. Sometimes a terminal moraine acts as a dam. McDonald, Bowman, and Kintla Lakes were formed when glaciers melted behind terminal moraines.

When two glaciers carve at opposite sides of a mountain, they cut ridges, or *aretes,* like the Garden Wall. If three or more glaciers grind away at several sides of a mountain, they carve a *horn* like Reynolds Mountain.

A *cirque* is a "bowl" carved out of a mountainside. Iceberg Lake near Many Glacier is in a glacier-carved cirque.

Lakes, aretes, cirques, and horns are some of the glacial features in this scenic park.

Hikers On A Terminal Moraine

Bowman Lake

Reynolds Mountain

Iceberg Lake

To Know a Glacier

No one should go on a glacier alone. There are deep cracks in glaciers called crevasses. Sometimes, even in July, a snow bridge can hide a dangerous, deep crevasse. A Ranger or glacier expert can show visitors where it's safe to walk. So to know a glacier, go with a Ranger-naturalist on a guided tour of Sperry or Grinnell Glacier.

It takes two days to see Sperry Glacier. You need a permit to camp four miles from the glacier, or a reservation to stay at Sperry Chalet. From Lake McDonald Lodge, you hike to the chalet or campground, spend the night, then hike to the glacier.

The all-day hike to Grinnell Glacier leaves from Many Glacier almost every day in midsummer.

Once on the glacier, you'll see ice tables, cones, and caves. You'll learn about other ice formations with strange names like *moulin, neve,* and *firn.*

On the way down, you'll see how the glacier-ground rock powder has made some lakes the color of turquoise. You'll enjoy the scenery carved by glaciers millions of years ago.

Crevasse—Grinnell Glacier

Turquoise Blue Lakes— Grinnell, Josephine, Sherburne

Mountain Goats

Glaciers did more than carve scenery. They carved a good home for mountain goats living here today. The glacier made steep cliffs where many animals cannot live easily. But the mountain goat is adapted to the steep cliffs and the cold of the mountain.

A thick woolly coat helps the goat adapt to the deep freeze of winter. Mountain goats' feet have flexible hoofs so they can walk on crusty snow and ice without slipping. Each flexible hoof surrounds a spongy pad that helps the animal cling to the rocks.

Even the icy wind is the mountain goat's friend. It blows snow off the ledges where sedges, grasses, lichen, and mosses provide a food supply. The goat can climb out to the smallest, farthest point to nibble lichen and moss from the rocks.

In summer, hikers on Gunsight Pass Trail may see goats. You may also see them on Mt. Oberlin near Logan Pass. Natural salt in the ground at Walton Goat Lick sometimes brings mountain goats down from their cliff homes.

Mountain Goat—A Symbol Of Glacier National Park ▶

Survival of Mountain Goats

Everything a mountain goat does helps the herd survive. It has adapted to cliffs so it has few natural enemies except mountain storms and avalanches.

In early June a female, or nanny, has one baby, a kid. Nannies keep the best feeding ranges for themselves and their kids. The kids must survive to grow up and have kids of their own. This means the males, or billies, have to look somewhere else for food.

Mountain goats stay in small groups most of the time. This way an avalanche would kill only a small part of the herd. In winter snowstorms, three or four goats can find shelter and enough to eat.

Big groups crowd a ledge, and kids might fall. So just a nanny, her newborn kid, and often a two-year-old stay together.

Nannies usually try to stay between danger and the kids. Danger might mean the edge of a cliff. It might mean a person with a camera.

Some hunters outside the park like to have mountain goats among their trophies. Then death comes from a rifle shot. Maybe falls, freezing, and avalanches are not the mountain goat's only enemies.

Mountain Goats Can Climb Steep Cliffs

A Nanny Stands Between Her Kid And Danger

Bighorn Sheep

Another high-country animal is the Rocky Mountain bighorn sheep. In summer the males, or rams, live high in the mountains. Females, or ewes, and their lambs graze in lower places like Many Glacier and Waterton's Red Rock Canyon.

In fall, ewes join the rams on the valley slopes. Then the rams fight to see which ones will win ewes. Often, two rams stand about 20 feet apart and get ready to battle. Heads down with horns aimed at each other, they run full speed and crash their curled horns together in a loud, hollow "clomp." Over and over again, they crash together in a battle that ends when one ram gives up and walks away.

The strongest rams win ewes for mating. The lambs from this mating are usually strong like the winning rams.

Hikers on the Highline Trail often see rams near Haystack Butte. Bighorns may come close to you but won't let you touch them. For safety, follow the rule, "Look, but don't touch."

Bighorn Ram ►

Please Don't Kill the Animals

"Look, but don't feed" is another good rule with any wildlife. The cute little squirrels sit up and beg because they want the salt on people's food. It's hard not to feed them when their dark eyes seem to say, "Give me a snack."

Animals, big and small, are happy to eat whatever visitors give them. But then they get lazy and forget how to find food for themselves.

Glacier National Park has an eight-month winter with deep snow. Few visitors are here to give crackers and nuts to the marmots, deer, and chipmunks. If animals have been fed the wrong kind of food all summer, they may not do well in winter. They may even die.

When Rangers say, "Please don't feed the animals," they may really be saying, "Please don't kill the animals."

Even if you drop a salty plastic potato chip bag, some animal might eat it. One moose cow died from eating too many plastic bags. What do you suppose happened to her calf?

Golden-Mantled Ground Squirrel Begs

Hoary Marmot

Chipmunk

Deer, Elk, and Moose

You see mule deer in many places at Glacier. White-tail deer browse on grass, shrubs, and small trees in valleys and burned areas like those near Camas Creek Road.

About 2000 elk roam the high forests until deep winter snow drives them to lower elevations.

Moose may be easier to find. Look for them in Waterton at Cameron Lake and Red Rock Canyon. Or you may see them near Lake McDonald at Moose Country. Late in the day they come to eat water lilies and pondweed growing on and under the water. They also eat cottonwoods, willows, and mountain maple.

Moose are the largest members of the deer family. The male, or bull moose, can weigh 1000 pounds or more. He has antlers, but the female, or cow, has none. She usually has one reddish brown calf in the spring.

Their very long legs help them move through water and deep snow. Great strength and sharp hoofs give good protection against other animals.

Moose Cow ►

Birds

If you watch carefully, you'll see many kinds of birds in Waterton-Glacier. Birds find nesting places in forests near lakes, ponds, and streams. Prairies in and around the park provide homes for grassland nesters. Hundreds of miles of streams and waterfalls attract the water ouzel. This little gray bird dives for insects at the bottom of fast-moving streams. You may find the ouzel at Baring Falls on the Sun Point Trail along the shore of St. Mary Lake.

In Logan Pass you must look carefully along the trail to Hidden Lake to find the Glacier Park bird. It's the white-tailed ptarmigan (tar mi gan), a small grouse. In summer the ptarmigan has tan, brown, and white feathers that help it hide among the rocks. As winter comes, it grows new white feathers. It's the only bird that lives in the high country all year.

From mid-June into July a mother ptarmigan sits on four to six eggs. For about 22 days she hardly leaves her nest as she waits for the chicks to hatch.

Water Ouzel Or Dipper

White-Tailed Ptarmigan

Bald Eagles

Some bald eagles live in the North Fork area of Glacier. The young, or immature, eagle is all brown. At about seven years, the mature eagle has a pure white head and tail.

If you visit Glacier in autumn, you can watch more than 300 bald eagles migrating to McDonald Creek. They come every year when thousands of kokanee salmon migrate from Flathead Lake to McDonald Creek near Apgar.

Each autumn, four-year-old salmon swim up the creek to spawn (lay eggs and fertilize them). After spawning, the salmon die. As soon as the first kokanee swim into the creek, eagles begin a daily flight to the banks and nearby trees.

Just before sunrise the eagles appear. When there's enough light to see, they swoop down and grab the dying fish with their claws, or talons. After they've eaten, the eagles bathe in the creek. Then they sit in the trees and comb their feathers with their beaks. Later, just before sunset, they fly off to their roosts about two miles away.

Immature Bald Eagle

Mature Bald Eagles Have White Heads And Tails

Bald Eagles Come When Kokanee Salmon Spawn

Bears

Two kinds of bears live in Glacier National Park: black bears and grizzly bears. How can you tell the difference?

Black bear is a kind of bear, not a color. It may be brown, reddish brown, black, or blond. A grizzly bear is brown or blond, and old ones look gray.

The biggest black bear is about 500 pounds. Grizzlies get as big as 800 pounds. A black bear has longer pointed ears and no tail. A grizzly has small round ears and a small tail. Long back legs make the black bear look as if it's going down hill. The grizzly has a big hump of strong shoulder muscles because it's a digger.

One joke says you can tell the difference between a black bear and a grizzly by climbing a tree. If the bear chases you up the tree, it's a black bear. If it knocks the tree down, it's a grizzly bear.

In winter, a bear sleeps most of the time in a den and lives off the fat it has made in the summer.

Cubs are born in February, usually in twos. Each baby weighs less than a pound, has no fur, and its eyes are closed.

A Black Bear May Be Brown, Reddish Brown, Black, Or Blond ►

Bear Country

In May bears come out of their dens. Mother bears teach their cubs where to find food and how to swim and climb trees. (Baby grizzlies climb trees until they get too big.) When the cubs are about two years old, their mother chases them away and goes to look for a mate. Now the cubs must take care of themselves.

Grizzly bears like to walk on bear trails, but they like people trails, too. They also have weak eyes. So unless they smell you or hear you, they won't know if you're coming along the same trail. To keep from surprising bears, hikers wear bells to let them know humans are coming.

If you surprise a bear, be quiet and don't move. It may go away. If it comes toward you, lie down on your stomach and put your hands over the back of your neck. Play dead, even if the bear hits or bites. If you fight, the bear will fight harder.

The sound of talking, laughing, and bells can keep you from surprising a bear. In fact, you'll be lucky if you even see one.

Glacier Is One Of The Last Homes Of The Grizzly Bear ►

Eco-Treks

If you're 18 or older, you can go on an Eco-Trek. On this three-day hike with a Ranger, you learn more about bears and how to take care of the wilderness.

Food smells attract bears, so you try to keep yourself and your campsite clean. After cooking, you wrap all your food carefully and hang it high in a tree far away from your tent. Then if a bear comes, it will go for the food instead of you—unless your face, hands, or clothes smell of food.

Thousands of people go into the backcountry every year, and each person hopes to find a true wilderness. So it's important to leave a campsite better than you find it. A tent can destroy grass in a meadow, so Eco-Trekkers camp on bare ground. They carry out all their own trash and stay on the trail. A small camping stove cooks food better than a wood fire and leaves no trace.

There are about eight Eco-Treks every summer. You bring your own food and equipment on this free hike. To go on an Eco-Trek, write to the Superintendent long before your visit. (See page 6.)

Eco-Trek In Glacier National Park

A Small Stove Leaves No Trace

Trails

You'll see more of Waterton-Glacier if you hike the trails. There are over 700 miles of trails and many guided walks. You can take a short, one-hour walk, a half-day, all-day, or even a three-day hike. You can go on your own or with a Ranger and a group of people. You may learn to know a fir from a spruce tree or what plants the elk and deer like to eat.

At Visitor Centers in Glacier, you can get a map and small newspaper with schedules for each part of the park. Ask at the Information Centre in Waterton for a map and schedule of programs and guided walks.

Self-guided walks are everywhere. At the beginning of some trails, you'll find pamphlets with numbered paragraphs. As you walk, look for numbered stakes. Then read about trees, plants, rocks, and other things you see.

Here are some hikes you shouldn't miss.

- Trail of Cedars near Avalanche Campground
- Hidden Lake Overlook Trail–Logan Pass
- Swiftcurrent Lake at Many Glacier
- Sun Point Nature Trail–St. Mary Lake
- Bear's Hump and Red Rock Canyon–Waterton

A Ranger Explains Flinsch Peak, A Horn

See The Garden Wall From Highline Trail

Avalanche Lake

Flowers

The Alpine Meadow at Logan Pass is famous for its wild flowers. There you'll see glacier lilies, pink meadowsweet, and many more.

Butter and eggs is a tall, bright yellow flower that grows in the valleys. It was brought here from Europe and now grows all over North America.

Beargrass, known as the Glacier Park flower, is not what its name says. Bears don't eat it, and it's not a grass but a lily. The showy white bloom grows as high as four feet out of a clump of grass-like leaves.

Some Indians used these grass-like leaves to weave baskets. They also used boiled beargrass roots to treat broken bones and sprains and to stop bleeding. When the flower turns to seed, it makes pods the Indians cooked for eating.

Beargrass blooms in early summer at low elevations near Lake McDonald. As the summer goes on, beargrass blooms are found higher and higher all the way to Logan Pass.

Glacier Lily

Butter And Eggs

Beargrass—A Symbol Of Glacier National Park

Trees

Trees do more than make the forest green. They provide homes for birds, food for insects, and shade for picnics.

Some tree roots hold the soil so it won't wash away in heavy rains. Other tree roots push at rocks and help break them down into soil.

Trees protect themselves with a layer of bark. The birch tree's bark is thin and peels off in curls. The larch's bark is thick and protects it from fire.

Leaves use sunlight, gases, and water to make food for the tree. Needles are leaves, and trees with needles are called evergreen because they stay green all year. Spruces, firs, and most pines are evergreens.

One member of the pine family, the larch, is not like most pines. Pines usually have long needles growing in bundles of five or less. The larch has short needles growing out of small twigs in groups of 30 or 40. These needles don't stay green all year but turn yellow in the fall. Every year, larches paint Glacier's slopes a bright gold before they drop their needles for winter.

Trees Do More Than Make Forests Green—McDonald Creek

Larch, Or Tamarack, In Fall

Fire

We do our best to keep from starting forest fires. But some fires are caused by lightning.

Any fire changes the land. Sometimes a lightning fire burns away underbrush before it gets thick enough to cause bigger fires. Fire gets rid of old and diseased trees and lets a whole new cycle begin. The food, or nutrients, in a log are turned to ashes. Then water carries the nutrients into the soil where they will feed new plants. After a burn, the tightly closed lodgepole pine cone opens up and lets go of its seeds.

Fire makes openings for sun-loving plants. These new plants provide a food supply for a whole new cycle of wildlife. Small animals and birds find food and a place to nest. They, in turn, may become a food supply for coyotes and other animals.

After a fire, aspens and willows spring up from old, underground root systems. Then moose, elk, and white-tailed deer can browse on the tender shoots.

On the Huckleberry Mountain Fire Ecology Trail, you'll see how fire is an important part of nature's cycle of life.

New Growth Begins After A Fire—
Huckleberry Mountain Fire Ecology Trail ▶

Winter

What happens in Glacier National Park during the eight-month winter, when only skiers brave the snow? Do squirrels starve? Don't frogs freeze?

No, because millions of snowflakes make a blanket on the ground. The snow blanket may be 10, 20, even 30 feet deep at higher elevations. Like feathers in a quilt, snowflakes trap dead air and make layers of insulation. Temperatures under this insulation can be 50 degrees warmer than the air above the snow.

Beneath a silent blanket, crickets, bumblebees, caterpillars, and wood frogs snuggle in leaf mold and pine needles. Ground squirrels and marmots hibernate in deep burrows. In dens, mother bears give birth to tiny, furless babies. By May they have nursed the cubs to ten-pound bundles of furry life.

Above ground, deer can reach more branches and twigs bent low by the weight of snow. Rabbits use ladders of drifted snow to get to bark and twigs they couldn't reach in summer

Life goes on through winter while you stay home and dream of Waterton-Glacier International Peace Park.

Skiers Brave The Snow

Life Goes On Under A Snow Blanket

Other Parks in Alberta and Montana

The same forces that shaped Waterton and Glacier carved the scenery of two other parks in Alberta, Canada. BANFF and JASPER NATIONAL PARKS offer towering peaks, lakes, and streams for hiking, camping, fishing, and boating.

ELK ISLAND NATIONAL PARK is near Edmonton in Alberta, Canada. This park is named for the large herds of wapiti, or elk, that once lived there. Among the gently rising, forested hills, many bison, or buffalo, graze between lakes and ponds.

WOOD BUFFALO is Canada's biggest national park. Here on the border between Alberta and Northwest Territories, bison run free. This vast prairie is the nesting place of the last wild flock of whooping cranes.

YELLOWSTONE NATIONAL PARK stretches across the borders between Wyoming, Idaho, and Montana. It's a wonderland of spouting geysers, colorful hot springs, and other strange features.

Banff National Park

Jasper National Park

Elk Island National Park

Yellowstone National Park

The Author and Illustrator

Wyoming-born Ruth Radlauer's love affair with National Parks began in Yellowstone. During her younger years she spent her summers in the Bighorn Mountains, in Yellowstone, or in the mountains near Casper.

Ed and Ruth Radlauer, graduates of the University of California at Los Angeles, are authors of many books for young people. Their subjects range from social studies to youth activities such as horse riding and motorcycles.

The Radlauers live in California, where they spend most of their time in the mountains near Los Angeles.

Photographing the national parks is a labor of love for Rolf Zillmer and his wife Evelyn. Because they are backpackers and wildlife enthusiasts, the Zillmers can give a truly intimate view of each park.

A former student at Art Center College of Design in Los Angeles, Mr. Zillmer was born in New York City. He now makes his home in Missoula, Montana, where he does painting, sculpture, and most of the art direction for Elk Grove Books.